CAT TALK

CAT TALK

Ariel Books

**Andrews McMeel
Publishing**

Kansas City

ISBN: 0-7407-0983-6

Library of Congress Catalog Card Number: 00-100472

INTRODUCTION

*Cats are mysterious beings . . . You never know if they love you
or if they condescend to occupy your house. This mystery is what makes
them the most attractive beast.*

PAUL MOORE

The cat's out of the bag: there's something about felines
that makes otherwise normal people gush. Written by cat
lovers for cat lovers, this charming volume collects the best

anecdotes, musings, poems, proverbs, fascinating facts, and quips about our precious pussies.

What is it about these mysterious mousers that inspires people to take pen to paper? Perhaps it's their indomitability, their refusal to learn tricks or to be put on a leash; perhaps it's their unpredictability, their ability to transform from a loving ball of fur into a whirling dervish of fury in the flick of a whisker. But most likely it's their beauty, mystery, and grace that draws us to them.

Cats were worshipped by ancient Egyptians, who considered them gods, built them temples, and mummified them. Later, however, cats were not so lucky. The same enigmatic quality so revered by the Egyptians became suspect in the Middle Ages. Cats became associated with the rites of pagan religions, especially witchcraft, and were persecuted mercilessly. But, they survived the hard times (having nine lives helped) and are worshipped once again, not as gods or goddesses, but as loving companions who fascinate, charm, and entertain us. As Colette said, "Our perfect companions never have fewer than four feet."

A cat improves the garden wall in sun—shine, and the hearth in foul weather.

JUDITH MERKLE RILEY

If stretching were wealth, the cat would be rich.

AFRICAN PROVERB

I love cats because
I enjoy my home; and
little by little, they
become its visible soul.

JEAN COCTEAU

The smallest feline

is a masterpiece.

LEONARDO DA VINCI

Prowling his own quiet backyard or asleep by the fire, he is still only a whisker away from the wilds.

JEAN BURDEN

Cats don't like change without their consent.

ROGER A. CARAS

Let the female cat run; the tomcat will catch her.

GERMAN PROVERB

LICK AND LET LICK

After being handled, cats lick themselves to
smooth out their fur and get rid of that
"person" smell. Licking is also thought to
produce a calming effect.

A cat is a tiger
that is fed by hand.

YAKAOKA GENRIN

Whenever the cat of the house is black, the lasses of lovers will have no lack.

FOLK SAYING

A cat is a lion
in a jungle of small
bushes.

INDIAN PROVERB

Another cat? Perhaps. For love there is also a season; its seeds must be resown. But a family cat is not replaceable like a wornout coat or a set of tires. Each new kitten becomes its own cat, and none is repeated. I am four cats old, measuring out my life in friends that have succeeded but not replaced one another. ❧

IRVING TOWNSEND

19

Cats are rather delicate creatures and
they are subject to a good many different
ailments, but I never heard of one
who suffered from insomnia.

JOSEPH WOOD KRUTCH

I am as vigilant as a
cat to steal cream.

WILLIAM SHAKESPEARE, *HENRY IV*

When she walked . . . she stretched out long and thin like a little tiger, and held her head high to look over the grass as if she were threading the jungle.

SARAH ORNE JEWETT

If you want to know
the character of a man,
find out what his cat
thinks of him.

ANONYMOUS

CAT✿FACT

Not every cat gets "high" from catnip, an herb belonging to the mint family. Whether or not a cat responds to it depends upon a recessive gene: no gene, no joy.

Of all the toys available, none is better designed than the owner himself. A large multipurpose plaything, its parts can be made to move in almost any direction. It comes completely assembled and it makes a sound when you jump on it. ❧

STEPHEN BAKER

The cat laps
moonbeams in the
bowl of water,
thinking them
to be milk.

HINDU PROVERB

Some pussies' coats are yellow; some amber streaked
    with dark;
No member of the feline race but has a special mark.
This one has feet with hoarfrost tipped; that one has
    tail that curls;
Another's inky hide is striped; another's decked
    with pearls. 🐛

ANONYMOUS

CAT 🐾 FACT

Cats were so revered in ancient Egypt that
all family members would shave their
eyebrows as a sign of mourning when
the family cat died.

A catless writer is almost inconceivable. It's a perverse taste, really, since it would be easier to write with a herd of buffalo in the room than even one cat; they make nests in the notes and bite the end of the pen and walk on the typewriter keys. 🐾

BARBARA HOLLAND

Curiosity killed
the cat,
Satisfaction brought
it back!

ENGLISH PROVERB

If I called her she would pretend not to hear, but would come a few moments later when it could appear that she had thought of doing so first.

ARTHUR WEIGALL

Even the stupidest cat
seems to know more
than any dog.

ELEANOR CLARK

A cat sneezing is a good omen for every-one who hears it.

ITALIAN SUPERSTITION

Catnip is vodka and whisky to most cats.

CARL VAN VECHTEN

A feline in a hurry can sprint at about thirty-one miles per hour.

Cats and monkeys,
monkeys and cats—
all human life is there.

HENRY JAMES

Cats are a mysterious kind of folk—
there is more passing in their minds
than we are aware of.

SIR WALTER SCOTT

Because his long
white whiskers tickled,
I began every day
laughing.

JANET F. FAURE

A cat's rage is beautiful, burning
with pure cat flame, all its hair standing
up and crackling blue sparks,
eyes blazing and sputtering.

WILLIAM S. BURROUGHS

Ye shall not possess any beast, my dear sisters, except only a cat.

THE ANCREN RIEWLE [NUN'S RULE]

WHERE'S THE BEEF?

Cats are not vegetarians and should never be
put on a vegetarian diet. Cats are flesh eaters
and need to eat meat.

I t's going to freeze,"
she would say,
" the cat's dancing."

❧

COLETTE

Cats are designated friends.

NORMAN CORWIN

A cat may look
at a king.

ENGLISH PROVERB

They sleep in the bed and go in and out of the cat door all night—I shudder to think what the laundry thinks we do to our sheets, because it's a sea of mud some nights. If they go in and out a lot all you get are little black pawprints. 🐾

SIAN PHILLIPS

Animals are not brethren,
they are not underlings; they are other
nations, caught with ourselves in
the net of life and time.

HENRY BESTON

No one likes to bell the cat.

GERMAN PROVERB

If animals could speak, the dog would be a blundering, outspoken, honest fellow—but the cat would have the rare grace of never saying a word too much.

PHILIP GILBERT HAMERTON

Our perfect
companions never have
fewer than four feet.

COLETTE

A cat may go to a monastery, but she still remains a cat!

❧

AFRICAN PROVERB

The most popular feline monikers in the United States:
Males: Smokey, Tiger, Max, Charlie, Rocky, Tigger, Sam/Sammy, Mickey, Toby
Females: Samantha, Misty, Muffin, Fluffy, Patches, Punkin, Missy, Tabitha, Tigger ❧

CAT FANCY MAGAZINE

My cats are compromised.
I do not entirely trust them—they may be
spies, like dolphins, reporting to some
unknown authority.

JAN MORRIS

I called my cat William because no shorter name fits the dignity of his character. Poor old man, he has fits now, so I call him fitz-William.

JOSH BILLINGS

The ideal of calm
exists in a sitting cat.

JULES REYNARD

CAT 🐾 FACT

An adult cat has thirty teeth and
about twelve whiskers.

They say the test of literary power is whether a man can write an inscription. I say, "Can he name a kitten?"

SAMUEL BUTLER

Most cats do not approach humans recklessly. The possibility of concealed weapons, clods or sticks, tends to make them reserved. Homeless cats in particular—with some justification, unfortunately—consider humans their natural enemies. Much ceremony must be observed, and a number of diplomatic feelers put out, before establishing a state of truce. ✌

LLOYD ALEXANDER

The Kilkenny Cats

There wanst was two cats of Kilkenny.
And aich thought there was wan cat too

    many;

        So they quarrelled and fit,

        And they scratched and they bit,

        Till barrin' their nails

        And the tips of their tails,

Instead of two cats, there warn't any.

ANONYMOUS

The little furry buggers are just deep, deep wells you throw all your emotions into.

BRUCE SCHIMMEL

The cat has too much
spirit to have no heart.

ERNEST MENAULT

The cat is a good friend, only she scratches.

PORTUGUESE PROVERB

Of all animals, he alone attains the Contemplative Life. He regards the wheel of existence from without, like the Buddha. There is no pretense of sympathy about the cat. He lives alone, aloft, sublime, in a wise passiveness. 🐾

ANDREW LANG

As one who has long been a pushover for cats, I should like to offer a packet of color–fast, preshrunk advice: If a stray kitten bounds out of nowhere when you're taking a walk, mews piteously, and rubs a soft shoulder against your leg, flee to the hills until the danger is over. 🐾

MURRAY ROBINSON

It always gives me a
shiver when I see a cat
seeing what I can't see.

ELEANOR FARJEON

A cat pent up
becomes a lion.

ITALIAN PROVERB

Whene'er I felt my towering fancy fail,
I stroked her head, her ears, her tail,
And, as I stroked, improved my dying song
From the sweet notes of her melodious tongue.
Her purrs and mews so evenly kept time,
She purred in metre and she mewed in rhyme.

JOSEPH GREEN

Who can believe
that there is no soul
behind those
luminous eyes!

THÉOPHILE GAUTIER

67

If we treated everyone we meet
with the same affection we bestow
upon our favorite cat, they, too,
would purr.

MARTIN BUXBAUM

The dog for the man,
the cat for the woman.

ENGLISH PROVERB

The Cheshire Cat only grinned when it saw Alice. It looked good-natured, she thought: still it had *very* long claws and a great many teeth, so she felt it ought to be treated with respect.

LEWIS CARROLL

I wonder what goes through his mind when he sees us peeing in his water bowl.

PENNY WARD MOSER

I f a cat does something,
we call it instinct; if we do the same
thing, for the same reason,
we call it intelligence.

WILL CUPPY

Let sleeping cats lie.

FRENCH PROVERB

I named him Caesar,
so I could call him
Julia's Caesar.

JULIA PHILLIPS

If a fish is the movement of water
embodied, given shape, then a cat is a
diagram and pattern of subtle air.

❦

DORIS LESSING

Even if you have just destroyed a Ming vase, purr. Usually all will be forgiven.

LENNY RUBENSTEIN

B y and large,
people who enjoy teaching animals
to roll over will find themselves
happier with a dog.

BARBARA HOLLAND

For me, one of the
pleasures of cats'
company is their
devotion to bodily
comfort.

COMPTON MACKENZIE

Oh, a cat's a cat. Babou's only too long when he really wants to be. Are we even sure he's black? He's probably white in snowy weather, dark blue at night, and red when he goes to steal strawberries. ❧

COLETTE

A cat is a puzzle for which there is no solution.

HAZEL NICHOLSON

Most cats, when they are Out
want to be In, and vice versa,
and often simultaneously.

LOUIS J. CAMUTI, D.V.M.

A black cat dropped
soundlessly from a high wall,
like a spoonful of dark treacle,
and melted under a gate.

ELIZABETH LEMARCHAND

To err is human,
To purr is feline.

ROBERT BYRNE

The Dog gives himself
the Airs of a Cat.

SIR RICHARD STEELE

A kitten is so flexible that she is almost double; the hind parts are equivalent to another kitten with which the forepart plays. She does not discover that her tail belongs to her until you tread on it. ❧

HENRY DAVID THOREAU

I am indebted to the species of the cat for a particular kind of honorable deceit, for a great control over myself, for characteristic aversion to brutal sounds, and for the need to keep silent for long periods of time. ❧

COLETTE

CAT FACT

What did Julius Caesar, Henri II, Charles XI, and Napoleon have in common? Ailurophobia—fear of cats. This fear made these otherwise lionhearted men nearly faint in the presence of a feline.

Sleeping together is a euphemism

for people but tantamount

to marriage with cats.

MARGE PIERCY

Among human beings

a cat is merely a cat;

among cats a cat is a prowling

shadow in a jungle.

KAREL ČAPEK

I'm used to dogs. When you leave them in the morning they stick their nose in the door crack and stand there like a portrait until you turn the key eight hours later. A cat would never put up with that kind of rejection. When you returned, she'd stalk you until you dozed off and then suck the air out of your body. ❧

ERMA BOMBECK

DANGEROUS DANDER

People who suffer from red eyes and sneezing when around cats are allergic to their dander—a combination of the feline's hair, saliva, and skin. Children who are allergic to cats may outgrow the condition.

If by chance I seated myself to write, she very slyly, very tenderly, seeking protection and caresses, would softly take her place on my knee and follow the comings and goings of my pen—sometimes effacing, with an unintentional stroke of her paw, lines of whose tenor she disapproved. ❧

PIERRE LOTI

PRECIOUS MEWTALS

Silver Tabby

Shaded Silver

Pewter

Golden Persian

Cream Silver Tabby

Silver-Patched Tabby

Blue Silver-Patched Tabby

Platinum

Bronze

The cat lives alone, has no need of society, obeys only when she pleases, pretends to sleep that she may see the more clearly, and scratches everything on which she can lay her paw. ❧

FRANÇOIS RENÉ DE CHATEAUBRIAND

It is bad luck to see a
white cat at night.

AMERICAN SUPERSTITION

When the cat and mouse agree, the grocer is ruined.

IRANIAN PROVERB

Do you see that kitten chasing so prettily her own tail? If you could look with her eyes, you might see her surrounded with hundreds of figures performing complex dramas, with tragic and comic issues, long conversations, many characters, many ups and downs of fate. ෴

RALPH WALDO EMERSON

The cat lets Man support her. But unlike the dog, she is no handlicker. Furthermore, unlike Man's other great good friend, the horse, the cat is no sweating serf of Man. The only labor she condescends to perform is to catch mice and rats, and that's fun. 🐭

VANCE PACKARD

The first cat show was held in London's
Crystal Palace in 1871. Nowadays,
over seventy-five thousand cats (and their
owners) claw for top honors at the more
than three hundred cat shows held in
the United States every year.

The problem with cats is that
they get the exact same look on their
face whether they see a moth or
an ax–murderer.

PAULA POUNDSTONE

But a cat can't eat a bone or any solid food on a polished surface. When a cat takes a bone off a plate and puts it down on the carpet before eating it, she's told she's dirty. But the cat needs to hold it down with her paw while she crunches and tears it and she can only do it on bare earth or on a carpet. People don't know this. ❧

COLETTE

Cats have intercepted my footsteps at the ankle for so long that my gait, both at home and on tour, has been compared to that of a man wading through low surf.

ROY BLOUNT, JR.

Of all God's creatures
there is only one that cannot
be made the slave of the lash.
That one is the cat.

MARK TWAIN

Cats everywhere
asleep on the
bookshelves like
motorized bookends.

AUDREY THOMAS

A child is a person who can't understand why someone would give away a perfectly good kitten.

DOUG LARSON

By associating with
the cat one only risks
becoming richer.

COLETTE

Purring would seem to be, in her case,
an automatic safety—valve device for
dealing with happiness overflow.

MONICA EDWARDS

Cats are smarter than dogs. You can't get eight cats to pull a sled through snow.

JEFF VALDEZ

When you see a one-eyed cat,
spit on your thumb, stamp it in the palm
of your hand, and make a wish.
The wish will come true.

AMERICAN SUPERSTITION.

Let take a cat, and foster him well with milk
And tender flesh and make his couch of silk,
And let him seen a mouse go by the wall,
Anon he waveth milk and flesh and all,
And every dainty that is in that house,
Such appetite he hath to eat a mouse. ❧

CHAUCER

Most beds sleep up to six cats. Ten cats without the owner.

STEPHEN BAKER

With the qualities of cleanliness, discretion, affection, patience, dignity, and courage that cats have, how many of us, I ask you, would be capable of being cats?

FERNAND MÉRY

A meow massages
the heart.

STUART MCMILLAN

ON A CAT AGING

He blinks upon the hearth-rug
And yawns in deep content,
Accepting all the comforts
That Providence has sent.

Louder he purrs and louder,
In one glad hymn of praise
For all the night's adventures,
For quiet, restful days.

Life will go on forever,
With all that cat can wish;
Warmth, and the glad procession
Of fish and milk and fish.

Only the thought disturbs him—
He's noticed once or twice,
That times are somehow breeding
A nimbler race of mice. ꝏ

SIR ALEXANDER GRAY

A cat has absolute emotional
honesty: human beings, for one reason
or another, may hide their feelings,
but a cat does not.

ERNEST HEMINGWAY

If a cat washes behind its ears, it will rain.

ENGLISH SUPERSTITION

When I play with my cat
who knows whether I do not make her
more sport than she makes me?

MICHEL DE MONTAIGNE

Rub a cat's paws
with butter and it will
never leave home.

FOLK REMEDY

There is nothing sweeter than his peace
when at rest,
For there is nothing brisker than his life
when in motion.

CHRISTOPHER SMART

Cats can be very funny,

and have the oddest ways of showing

they're glad to see you.

Rudimace always peed in our shoes.

W. H. AUDEN

She sights a Bird—she chuckles—
She flattens—then she crawls—
She runs without the look of feet—
Her eyes increase to Balls.

EMILY DICKINSON

There is no more
intrepid explorer than
a kitten.

JULES CHAMPFLEURY

CAT FACT

A group of youngsters is called a *kindle;*
those old-timers form a *clowder.*

As I was going to St. Ives,
I met a man with seven wives,
Each wife had seven sacks,
Each sack has seven cats,
Each cat had seven kits:
Kits, cats, sacks, wives,
How many were going to St. Ives?

NURSERY RHYME

Cats are a waste
of fur.

RITA RUDNER

He seems the incarnation of
everything soft and silky and velvety,
without a sharp edge in his composition,
a dreamer whose philosophy is
sleep and let sleep . . .

SAKI

Cats always know whether
people like or dislike them.
They do not always care enough to
do anything about it.

WINIFRED CARRIERE

Dogs come when
they're called;
cats take a message and
get back to you.

MARY BLY

Always the cat remains a little beyond the limits we try to set for him in our blind folly.

ANDRE NORTON

VERSES ON A CAT

1 A cat in distress,
    Nothing more, nor less;
Good folks, I must faithfully tell ye,
    As I am a sinner,
    It waits for some dinner
To stuff out its own little belly.

2 You would not easily guess
    All the modes of distress
Which torture the tenants of earth;
    And the various evils,
    Which like so many devils,
Attend the poor souls from their birth.

3 Some a living require,
    And others desire
An old fellow out of the way;
    And which is the best
    I leave to be guessed,
For I cannot pretend to say.

4 ❧ One wants society,
   Another variety,
Others a tranquil life;
   Some want food.
   Others, as good,
Only want a wife.

            5 ❧ But this poor little cat
               Only wanted a rat,
         To stuff out its own little maw;
               And it were as good
               Some people had such food,
         To make them hold their jaw. ❧

PERCY BYSSHE SHELLEY

The cat sees through
shut lids.

ENGLISH PROVERB

It is in their eyes that their magic resides.

ARTHUR SYMONS

They smell and they snarl and they scratch; they have a singular aptitude for shredding rugs, drapes, and upholstery; they're sneaky, selfish, and not particularly smart; they are disloyal, condescending, and totally useless in any rodent-free environment. ॐ

JEAN-MICHEL CHAPEREAU

A cat sleeping with all four paws tucked under means cold weather ahead.

ENGLISH SUPERSTITION

No matter how tired or wretched I am, a pussycat sitting in a doorway can divert my mind.

MARY E. WILKINS FREEMAN

Oh, the cats in this town have their secrets.

MARY VIRGINIA MICKA

A bashful cat makes
a proud mouse.

SCOTTISH PROVERB

Balanchine has trained his cat to perform brilliant *jetés* and *tours en l'air;* he says that at last he has a body worth choreographing for.

BERNARD TAPER

A dog is prose,
a cat is a poem.

JEAN BURDEN

Like those great sphinxes lounging
through eternity in noble attitudes upon
the desert sand, they gaze incuriously
at nothing, calm and wise.

CHARLES BAUDELAIRE

If only cats grew
into kittens.

R. D. STERN

The way to keep a cat
is to try to chase
it away.

E. W. HOWE

There are some who, if a cat accidentally comes into the room, though they will neither see it nor are told of it, will presently be in a sweat and ready to die away.

INCREASE MATHER

One [cat] is tabby with emerald eyes,
And a tail that's long and slender,
And into a temper she quickly flies
If you ever by chance offend her. ❧

THOMAS HOOD

CAT LORE

If you discover one white hair on an all-black cat, Lady Luck will smile on you; or so they think in France.

Cats, like women, should be
respected as individuals rather than
admired as decoration, but there's no
harm, given a choice, in taking up
with a strikingly attractive
specimen of either.

BARBARA HOLLAND

Black cat superstitions are as American as apple pie. In Asia and England, black cats are considered lucky.

God made the cat in order that man might have the pleasure of caressing the tiger.

FERNAND MÉRY

CAT 🐾 FACT

KITTY HOOK

A cat's tongue consists of small "hooks,"
which come in handy when tearing up food.

Cats are dangerous companions

for writers because cat watching

is a near-perfect method of

writing avoidance.

DAN GREENBURG

Two little kittens, one stormy night,
Began to quarrel, and then to fight;
One had a mouse, the other had none,
And that's the way the quarrel begun.

ANONYMOUS

If cats could talk, they wouldn't.

NAN PORTER

I have as companion a big greyish-red cat with black stripes across it. It was born in the Vatican, in the Raphael loggia. Leo XII brought it up in a fold of his robes where I had often looked at it enviously when the Pontiff gave me an audience.... It was called "the Pope's cat." In this capacity, it used to enjoy the special consideration of pious ladies. I am trying to make it forget exile, the Sistine Chapel, the sun on Michelangelo's cupola, where it used to walk, far above the earth. ❧

FRANÇOIS RENÉ DE CHATEAUBRIAND

A cat with kittens
nearly always decides
sooner or later to
move them.

SIDNEY DENHAM

TO A CAT

Stately, kindly, lordly friend,
  Condescend
Here to sit by me, and turn
Glorious eyes that smile and burn,
Golden eyes, love's lustrous meed,
On the golden page I read.

All your wondrous wealth of hair,
  Dark and fair,
Silken-shaggy, soft and bright
As the clouds and beams of night,
Pays my reverent hand's caress
Back with friendlier gentleness. ❧

ALGERNON SWINBURNE

Cats, even when robust, have scant
liking for the boisterous society
of children, and are apt to exert their
utmost ingenuity to escape it.

AGNES REPPLIER

We've got a cat
called Ben Hur.
We called it Ben till
it had kittens.

SALLY POPLIN

We quickly discovered that two kittens were much more fun than one.

ALLEN LACY

Way down deep, we're all motivated by the same urges. Cats have the courage to live by them.

JIM DAVIS

Such is one of those big-whiskered and well-furred tomcats, that you see quiet in a corner, digesting at his leisure, sleeping if it seems good to him, sometimes giving himself to the pleasure of hunting, for the rest enjoying life peaceably, without being troubled by restless reflections, and little caring to communicate his thoughts to others. Truly it needs only that a female cat come on the scene to derange all his philosophy; but are our philosophers any wiser on such occasions?

FATHER BOUGEANT

Artists like cats;
soldiers like dogs.

DESMOND MORRIS

The best thing about animals is that they don't talk much.

THORNTON WILDER

Cats are only
human, they have
their faults.

KINGSLEY AMIS

There is the little matter of disposal of droppings in which the cat is far ahead of his rivals. The dog is somehow thrilled by what he or any of his friends have produced, hates to leave it, adores smelling it, and sometimes eats it . . . The cat covers it up if it can . . . ❧

PAUL GALLICO

A cat's a cat and
that's that.

FOLK SAYING

A cat is the only domestic animal
I know who toilet trains itself and does a
damned impressive job of it.

JOSEPH EPSTEIN

Cats are the ultimate narcissists. You can tell this because of all the time they spend on personal grooming. Dogs aren't like this. A dog's idea of personal grooming is to roll in a dead fish.

JAMES GORMAN

Cats must have three names—an everyday name, such as Peter; a more particular, dignified name, such as Quaxo, Bombalurina, or Jellylorum; and, thirdly, the name the cat thinks up for himself, his deep and inscrutable singular Name. 🐾

T. S. ELIOT

A sleeping cat is
ever alert.

FRED SCHWAB

When it comes to the advantages of cats *versus* dogs as pets, there is no competition. Try going away for a weekend, leaving your German shepherd alone with a bowl of dry food, some water, and a litter box . . .

ROBERT STEARNS

Her function is to sit and be admired.

GEORGINA STRICKLAND GATES

In a cat's eyes, all
things belong to cats.

ENGLISH PROVERB

She sits composedly sentinel, with paws tucked under her, a good part of her days at present, by some ridiculous little hole, the possible entry of a mouse.

HENRY DAVID THOREAU

It is bad luck to cross a stream carrying a cat.

FRENCH SUPERSTITION

Vengeance I ask and cry,

By way of exclamation,

On the whole nation

Of cats wild and tame:

God send them sorrow and shame!

JOHN SKELTON

Every life should
have nine cats.

ANONYMOUS

A mouse in the paws
is worth two in
the pantry.

LOUIS WAIN

A scalded cat dreads
even cold water.

FRENCH PROVERB

For unlike a dog that will scare up a
flock of birds and then rush away,
a cat, even in bitter weather, will wait
patiently for hours hoping to make a kill.

THALASSA CRUSO

Dogs remember faces,
cats remember places.

ENGLISH PROVERB

Cat hate reflects an ugly, stupid, loutish, bigoted spirit.

WILLIAM S. BURROUGHS

Old cats mean young mice.

ITALIAN PROVERB

I've met many thinkers and many cats, but the wisdom of cats is infinitely superior.

HIPPOLYTE TAINE

To live long, eat like a cat, drink like a dog.

GERMAN PROVERB

If a cat spoke, it would say things like, "Hey, I don't see the problem here."

ROY BLOUNT, JR.

I shall never forget the indulgence with which he treated Hodge, his cat, for whom he used to go out and buy oysters, lest the servants having that trouble should take a dislike to the poor creature. . . . I recollect him one day scrambling up on Dr. Johnson's breast, apparently with much satisfaction, while my friend, smiling and half-whistling, rubbed his back and pulled him by the tail; and when I observed he was a fine cat, saying, "Why, yes, Sir, but I have had cats whom I liked better than this." And then as if perceiving Hodge to be out of countenance adding, "But he is a very fine cat, very fine cat indeed." ❧

JAMES BOSWELL

A cat is there when you call her—if she doesn't have something better to do.

BILL ADLER

The phrase
"domestic cat"
is an oxymoron.

GEORGE WILL

Wake not a sleeping cat.

FRENCH PROVERB

Pussy will rub my knees with her head

Pretending she loves me hard;

But the very minute I go to bed

Pussy runs out in the yard . . .

RUDYARD KIPLING

Never wear anything that panics the cat.

P. J. O'ROURKE

The cat loves fish, but hates wet feet.

ITALIAN PROVERB

An ordinary kitten
will ask more questions
than any
five year-old.

CARL VAN VECHTEN

Everything that moves, serves to interest and amuse a cat. He is convinced that nature is busying herself with his diversion; he can conceive of no other purpose in the universe.

F. A. PARADIS DE MONCRIF

All cats are grey in the dark.

ENGLISH PROVERB

Since each of us is blessed with only one life, why not live it with a cat?

ROBERT STEARNS

It's very hard to be
polite if you're a cat.

ANONYMOUS

No animal should ever jump upon
the dining-room furniture unless
absolutely certain he can hold his
own in the conversation.

FRAN LEBOWITZ

GROCERY LIST OF FUR COLORS

Cream

Chocolate Point

Chocolate Tortie

Blue Mackerel Tabby

Brown Mackerel Tabby

Cinnamon

Chestnut

Champagne

Honey Mink

Chocolate Tipped

Light Chocolate Tipped

Caramel

Caramel Silver-Ticked Tabby

Chestnut Spotted

An old cat will not
learn dancing.

MOROCCAN PROVERB

Passion for place—
there is no greater urge
in feline nature.

PAUL ANNIXTER

WHAT'S IN A NAME?

The silks created by weavers in Baghdad, Iraq were inspired by the beautiful and varied colors and markings of cat coats. These fabrics were called "tabby" by European traders.

203

He was sitting in front of the door. It is a known fact that if one sits long enough in front of a door, doing the proper yoga exercises, the door will open.

MAY SARTON

Cat people are different, to the extent
that they generally are not conformists.
How could they be, with a cat
running their lives?

LOUIS J. CAMUTI, D.V.M.

I soon realized the name Pouncer in no way did justice to her aerial skills. By the end of the first day I had amended her name to Kamikaze.

CLEVELAND AMORY

An old cat laps as much milk as a young.

ENGLISH PROVERB

what in hell
have i done to deserve
all these kittens

DON MARQUIS

Did St. Francis really preach to the birds? Whatever for? If he really liked birds he would have done better to preach to the cats.

REBECCA WEST

Acat has nine lives.
For three he plays, for three he strays,
and for the last three he stays.

ENGLISH AND AMERICAN
PROVERB

Those who'll play with cats must expect to be scratched.

MIGUEL DE CERVANTES

I saw the most beautiful cat today. It was sitting by the side of the road, its two front feet neatly and graciously together. Then it gravely swished around its tail to completely encircle itself. It was so *fit* and beautifully neat, that gesture, and so self-satisfied so complacent. 🐾

ANNE MORROW LINDBERGH

CAT🐾FACT

VIBRATING VIBRISSAE?

A cat's whiskers, called vibrissae, grow on the
cat's face as well as on the backs of its forelegs.
The whiskers are thought to be a kind of
radar, which helps a cat gauge the space it
intends to walk through. By the way, if a cat's
whiskers are cut off for any reason,
they *will* grow back.

If there is one spot of sun spilling onto the floor, a cat will find it and soak it up.

JOAN ASPER MCINTOSH

Cats find malicious amusement in doing what they know they are not wanted to do, and that with an affectation of innocence that materially aggravates their deliberate offense.

HELEN WINSLOW

A cat bitten once by
a snake dreads
even rope.

ARABIAN PROVERB

I love cats. I love their grace and their elegance. I love their independence and their arrogance, and the way they lie and look at you, summing you up, surely to your detriment, with that unnerving, unwinking, appraising stare. 🐾

JOYCE STRANGER

All cats are bad in May.

FRENCH PROVERB

Odd things animals.

All dogs look up to you.

All cats look down to you.

Only a pig looks at you as an equal.

WINSTON CHURCHILL

Calvin's life seems to me a fortunate one, for it was natural and unforced. He ate when he was hungry, slept when he was sleepy, and enjoyed existence to the very tips of his toes and the end of his expressive and slow-moving tail. 🐦

CHARLES DUDLEY WARNER

Who's that ringing at my doorbell?

A little pussy cat that isn't very well.

Rub its little nose with a little mutton fat,

That's the best cure for a little pussy cat.

NURSERY RHYME

A cat is a lion
to a mouse.

ALBANIAN PROVERB

Dearest cat, honoured guest of my
old house,
Arch your supple, tingling back,
And curl upon my knee, to let me
Bathe my fingers in your warm fur.

FRANÇOIS LEMAÎTRE

The trouble with cats
is that they've got
no tact.

P. G. WODEHOUSE

He's as honest as the cat when the meat is out of reach.

ENGLISH PROVERB

Acat in despondency sighed,
And resolved to commit suicide;
She passed under the wheels of eight
   automobiles,
And after the ninth one she died.

ANONYMOUS

226

Kittens are constantly forgiven.

DOUGLAS WILK

The playful kitten, with its pretty
little tigerish gambols, is infinitely more
amusing than half the people
one is obliged to live with
in the world.

LADY SYDNEY MORGAN

No amount of time can erase
the memory of a good cat,
and no amount of masking tape
can ever totally remove his fur
from your couch.

LEO DWORKEN

Confront a child, a puppy, and a kitten with sudden danger; the child will turn instinctively for assistance, the puppy will grovel in abject submission to the impending visitation, the kitten will brace its tiny body for a frantic resistance. ❧

SAKI

No one can have experienced to the fullest the true sense of achievement and satisfaction who has never pursued and successfully caught his tail.

ROSALIND WELCHER

CAT 🐾 FACT

Extra! Extra!—The Russian blue is a breed
prone to having an extra toe. Six-toed kitties
are so common in Boston and surrounding
parts of Massachusetts that some experts
consider it an established mutation.

One of the striking differences
between a cat and a lie is that
a cat has only nine lives.

MARK TWAIN

Most of us rather like our cats to have a streak of wickedness. I should not feel quite easy in the company of any cat that walked about the house with a saintly expression . . .

BEVERLY NICHOLS

The cat went here and there
And the moon spun round like a top,
And the nearest kin of the moon,
The creeping cat, looked up.
Black Minnaloushe stared at the moon,
For, wander and wail as he would,
The pure cold light in the sky
Troubled his animal blood.
Minnaloushe runs in the grass
Lifting his delicate feet.
Do you dance, Minnaloushe, do you dance? 🐦

WILLIAM BUTLER YEATS

Oh heaven will not ever Heaven be
Unless my cats are there to welcome me.

EPITAPH IN A PET CEMETERY

The thing that astonished him was that cats should have two holes cut in their coat exactly at the place where their eyes are.

GEORG CHRISTOPH
LICHTENBERG

At whiles it seems as if one were somewhat as the cats, which ever have appeared to me to be animals of two parts, the one of the house and the cushion and the prepared food, the other that is free of the night and runs wild with the wind in its coat and the smell of the earth in its nostrils. ❧

UNA L. SILBERRAD

THE CONSCIENCE OF A CAT

A dog will often steal a bone,
But conscience lets him not alone,
And by his tail his guilt is known.

> But cats consider theft a game
> And, howsoever you may blame,
> Refuse the slightest sign of shame.

When food mysteriously goes,
The chances are that Pussy knows
More than she leads you to suppose.

> And hence there is no need for you,
> If Puss declines a meal or two,
> To feel her pulse or make ado. ❧

ANONYMOUS

All animals are equal, but some animals are more equal than others.

GEORGE ORWELL

When the cat's away, the mice will play.

SAYING

We should be careful to get out of an experience only the wisdom that is in it and stop there; lest we be like the cat that sits on a hot stove lid. She will never sit down on a hot stove lid again and that is well; but also she will never sit down on a cold one any more. 🐾

MARK TWAIN

THE KITTEN AT PLAY

See the kitten on the wall,
Sporting with the leaves that fall,
Withered leaves, one, two,
    and three
Falling from the elder tree,
Through the calm and frosty air
Of the morning bright and fair.

See the kitten, how she starts,
Crouches, stretches, paws and
    darts,
With a tiger-leap half way
Now she meets her coming prey.
Lets it go as fast and then
Has it in her power again.

WILLIAM WORDSWORTH

My cat does not talk as respectfully to me as I do to her.

COLETTE

Every cat is really the most beautiful woman in the room.

E. V. LUCAS

The cat is truly
aristocratic in type
and origin.

ALEXANDRE DUMAS

The cat is a dilettante in fur.

THÉOPHILE GAUTIER

LONG-HAIRED WORLD TRAVELERS

Persian

Himalayan

Turkish Angora

Javanese

Maine Coon

Norwegian Forest

Siberian

Balinese

Cleanliness in the cat world is usually a virtue put above godliness.

CARL VAN VECHTEN

Cats are notoriously sore losers. Coming in second best, especially to someone as poorly coordinated as a human being, grates their sensibility.

STEPHEN BAKER

It is no easy task to win the friendship of a cat. He is a philosopher, sedate, tranquil, a creature of habit, a lover of decency and order. He does not bestow his regard lightly, and, though he may consent to be your companion, he will never be your slave. 🐦

THÉOPHILE GAUTIER

A cat is always on
the wrong side of
the door.

ANONYMOUS

Dreaming of
a white cat means
good luck.

AMERICAN SUPERSTITION

As soon as they're out of your sight, you are out of their mind.

WALTER DE LA MARE

Your cat will never threaten your popularity by barking at three in the morning. He won't attack the mailman or eat the drapes, although he may climb the drapes to see how the room looks from the ceiling.

HELEN POWERS

No matter how much cats fight, there always seem to be plenty of kittens.

ABRAHAM LINCOLN

Don't buy a cat in a sack.

DUTCH PROVERB

A home without a cat—and a well-fed, well-petted and properly revered cat—may be a perfect home, perhaps, but how can it prove its title?

MARK TWAIN

... Purring beside our fireplaces and pattering along our back fences, we have got a wild beast as uncowed and uncorrupted as any under heaven.

ALAN DEVOE

To bathe a cat takes brute force, perseverance, courage of conviction —and a cat. The last ingredient is usually hardest to come by.

STEPHEN BAKER

A dog is like a liberal.

He wants to please everybody.

A cat really doesn't need to know

that everybody loves him.

WILLIAM KUNSTLER

Pure herring oil
is the port wine of
English cats.

HONORÉ DE BALZAC

Cats don't bark and act brave when they see something small in fur or feathers, they kill it. Dogs tend to bravado. They're braggarts. In the great evolutionary drama the dog is Sergeant Bilko, the cat is Rambo. ❧

JAMES GORMAN

Cats hide their claws.

ENGLISH PROVERB

Do our cats name us? My former husband swore that Humphrey and Dolly and Bean Blossom called me The Big Hamburger.

ELEANORA WALKER

A friend complained to humorist Dorothy Parker that his cat had gotten so ill that he had no choice but to put his beloved pet to sleep. Yet still he was torn: How could he possibly kill his closest companion? "Try curiosity," quipped Parker.

Cats seldom make mistakes and they never make the same mistake twice.

CARL VAN VECHTEN

Some men are born to cats, others have cats thrust upon them.

GILBERT MILLSTEIN

Again I must
remind you that
A Dog's a Dog—
A CAT'S A CAT.

❧

T. S. ELIOT

WELL-TRAVELED
SHORT-HAIRED CATS

Japanese Bobtail	Burmese
Scottish Fold	Asian
European Shorthair	Bombay
Cornish Rex	Singapura
Devon Rex	Oriental Shorthair
Russian Shorthair	Egyptian Mau
Siamese	Abyssinian

He that denies the cat skimmed milk must give the mouse cream.

RUSSIAN PROVERB

Bathsheba:
To whom none ever said scat,
No worthier cat
Ever sat on a mat
Or caught a rat:
        Requies—cat. ⁊

JOHN GREENLEAF WHITTIER

Pussy cat, pussy cat,
    Where have you been?
I've been to London
    To look at the Queen.
Pussy cat, pussy cat,
    What did you there?
I frightened a little mouse
    Under her chair. 🐦

NURSERY RHYME

The best exercise for a
cat is another cat.

JO AND PAUL LOEB

IN HONOR OF TAFFY TOPAZ

Taffy, the topaz–coloured cat,
Thinks now of this and now
    of that,
But chiefly on his meals.
Asparagus, and cream, and fish,
Are objects of his Freudian wish;
What you don't give, he steals.

His amiable amber eyes
Are very friendly, very wise;
Like Buddha, grave and fat,
He sits, regardless of applause,
And thinking, as he kneads
    his paws,
What fun to be a cat! 🐾

CHRISTOPHER MORLEY

There is one respect in which
brutes show real wisdom when
compared with us—I mean
their quiet, placid enjoyment
of the present moment.

ARTHUR SCHOPENHAUER

There is something about the
presence of a cat . . . that seems
to take the bite out
of being alone.

LOUIS J. CAMUTI, D.V.M.

The tail, in cats, is the principal organ

of emotional expression,

and a Manx cat is the equivalent

of a dumb man.

❧ ❧

ALDOUS HUXLEY

When moving to a new home,
always put the cat through the
window instead of the door,
so that it will not leave.

AMERICAN SUPERSTITION

Rarely do you see a
cat discomfited. They
have no conscience,
and they never regret.

BARBARA WEBSTER

It [the Cheshire Cat] vanished quite
slowly, beginning with the end of
the tail, and ending with the grin,
which remained some time after
the rest of it had gone.

LEWIS CARROLL

At dinner time he would sit in a corner, concentrating, and suddenly they would say, "Time to feed the cat," as if it were their own idea.

LILIAN JACKSON BRAUN

Cats seem to go on
the principle that it
never does any harm to
ask for what you want.

JOSEPH WOOD KRUTCH

A cat can purr its way out of anything.

DONNA MCCROHAN

The cat does not offer services.
The cat offers itself. Of course he wants
care and shelter. You don't buy love
for nothing. Like all pure creatures,
cats are practical.

WILLIAM S. BURROUGHS

Meow is like aloha—it can mean anything.

HANK KETCHUM

Dear creature by the fire a-purr,
Strange idol, eminently bland,
Miraculous puss! As o'er your furr
I trail a negligible hand

And gaze into your gazing eyes,
And wonder in a demi-dream
What mystery it is that lies
Behind those slits that glare and gleam. . . . ❧

LYTTON STRACHEY

The more you rub a cat on the rump, the higher she sets her tail.

JOHN RAY

A cat is a
four-footed allergen.

THOMAS MAEDER

Cats are mysterious beings . . .

You never know if they love you or if they

condescend to occupy your house.

This mystery is what makes them

the most attractive beast.

PAUL MOORE

The great charm of cats is their rampant egotism, their devil-may-care attitude toward responsibility, their disinclination to earn an honest dollar.

ROBERTSON DAVIES

There are no ordinary cats.

COLETTE

No tame animal has lost less of its
dignity or maintained more of its ancient
reserve. The domestic cat might
rebel tomorrow.

WILLIAM CONWAY

A cat is never
vulgar.

CARL VAN VECHTEN

Cats are absolute individuals,

with their own ideas about everything,

including the people they own.

JOHN DINGMAN

It is too much to expect
of a cat that she should
sit by the milk and
not lap it.

GERMAN PROVERB

SONNET TO MRS. REYNOLDS' CAT

Cat! who hast pass'd thy grand climacteric,
  How many mice and rats hast in thy days
  Destroy'd How many tit-bits stolen? Gaze
With those bright languid segments green, and prick
Those velvet ears but pr'ythee do not stick
  Thy latent talons in me and upraise
  Thy gentle mew and tell me all thy frays
Of fish and mice, and rats and tender chick.
Nay, look not down, nor lick thy dainty wrists—
  For all the wheezy asthma, and for all
Thy tail's tip is nick'd off and though the fists
  Of many a maid have given thee many a maul,
Still is that fur as soft as when the lists
  In youth thou enter'dst on glass bottled wall. ❧

JOHN KEATS

Living with a cat is like being married to a career woman who can take domesticity or let it alone, so you'd better be nice to her.

MARGARET COOPER GAY

One of them likes to be crammed into a corner-pocket of the billiard table which he fits as snugly as does a finger in a glove and then he watches the game (and obstructs it) by the hour, and spoils many a shot by putting out his paw and changing the direction of a passing ball. Whenever a ball is in his arms, or so close to him that it cannot be played upon with risk of hurting him, the player is privileged to remove it to one of the 3 spots that chances to be vacant. ❧

MARK TWAIN

Time, that spoils all things, will,
I suppose, make her also a cat . . . For no
wisdom that she may gain by experience
and reflection hereafter will compensate
for the loss of her present hilarity.

WILLIAM COWPER

Dame Trot and her cat
Sat down for a chat;
The Dame sat on this side
And puss sat on that.

Puss, says the Dame
Can you catch a rat
Or a mouse in the dark?
Purr, says the cat. 🐾

NURSERY RHYME

The real objection to the great majority of cats is their insufferable air of superiority.

P. G. WODEHOUSE

You always ought to have

tomcats arranged, you know—

it makes 'em more companionable.

NOEL COWARD

$\ldots$ You are my cat
and I am your human.

HILAIRE BELLOC

I will always remember the olive-eyed tabby who taught me that not all relationships are meant to last a lifetime. Sometimes just an hour is enough to touch your heart. 🐾

BARBARA L. DIAMOND

A cat stretches
from one end of my
childhood to the other.

❦

BLAGA DIMITROVA

Two cats can live as cheaply as one, and their owner has twice as much fun.

LLOYD ALEXANDER

To escort a cat on a
leash is against the
nature of the cat.

ADLAI STEVENSON

When a Cat adopts you there is
nothing to be done about it except to
put up with it and wait until
the wind changes.

T. S. ELIOT

Even overweight cats
instinctively know the
cardinal rule: when
fat, arrange yourself
in slim poses.

JOHN WEITZ

When my cats aren't happy, I'm not happy. Not because I care about their mood but because I know they're just sitting there thinking up ways to get even.

PENNY WARD MOSER

Quite obviously a cat trusts
human beings; but she doesn't trust
another cat because she knows
better than we do.

KAREL ČAPEK

Why people should prefer a wet cat to a dry one I have never been able to understand; but that a wet cat is practically sure of being taken in and gushed over, while a dry cat is liable to have the garden hose turned upon it, is an undoubted fact. ❧

JEROME K. JEROME

As every cat owner knows, nobody owns a cat.

ELLEN PERRY BERKELEY

Happy owner,
happy cat.
Indifferent owner,
reclusive cat.

CHINESE PROVERB

Cat lovers can readily be identified. Their clothes always look old and well used. Their sheets look like bath towels and their bath towels look like a collection of knitting mistakes.

ERIC GURNEY

Cats are intended to
teach us that not
everything in nature
has a function.

GARRISON KEILLOR

It is impossible for a lover of cats to banish these alert, gentle, and discriminating friends, who give us just enough of their regard and complaisance to make us hunger for more.

AGNES REPPLIER

The cat has always been associated with the moon. Like the moon it comes to life at night, escaping from humanity and wandering over housetops with its eyes beaming out through the darkness.

PATRICIA DALE-GREEN

A dog is a dog,
a bird is a bird, and
a cat is a person.

MUGSY PEABODY

Kittens can happen to anyone.

PAUL GALLICO

He will kill Mice and he will be kind to Babies when he is in the house, as long as they do not pull his tail too hard. But when he has done that, and between times, he is the Cat that walks by himself and all places are alike to him, and if you look out at nights you can see him waving his wild tail and walking by his wild lone just the same as before. 🐾

RUDYARD KIPLING

If man could be
crossed with the cat, it
would improve man
but deteriorate the cat.

MARK TWAIN

TELL ME A TAIL

You don't need a pet psychiatrist to tell you
how your cat is feeling—just watch your
feline's tail. A tail held high means
happiness; a twitching tail is a warning sign,
and a tail tucked in close to the body
is a sure sign of insecurity.

I don't mind a cat, in its place. But its place is not in the middle of my back at 4 A.M.

MAYNARD GOOD STODDARD

Feline communicators divide naturally into two groups: acrobatic types who hang on the screen door when they want to come in, and the verbalizers who use yowling as a calling card.

LEO DWORKEN

I think that the reason we admire cats, those of us who do, is their proficiency in one-upmanship. They always seem to come out on top, no matter what they are doing—or pretend to be doing . . . Maybe we secretly envy them. 🐾

BARBARA WEBSTER

A kitten is the delight
of a household.
All day long a comedy is played
by this incomparable actor.

JULES CHAMPFLEURY

... Those dear, sweet little lumps, stumping, and padding about the house, pulling over electric lamps, making little puddles in slippers, crawling up my legs, on to my lap (my legs are scratched by them, like Lazarus's), I see myself finding a kitten in the sleeve when I'm putting on my coat, and my tie under the bed when I want to put it on . . . ❧

KAREL ČAPEK

A kitten is chiefly remarkable for rushing about like mad at nothing whatever, and generally stopping before it gets there.

AGNES REPPLIER

But buds will be roses,

and kittens, cats,

—more's the pity.

LOUISA MAY ALCOTT

Cats have a third eyelid, called a *haw*,
which is rarely visible. If it *is* visible, it could
be an indication of ill health.

I'll pat pretty pussy, and then she will purr;
And thus show her thanks for my kindness to her.
But I'll not pinch her ears, nor tread on her paw,
Lest I should provoke her to use her sharp claw.
I never will vex her, or make her displeased—
For pussy don't like to be worried and teased. 🍂

ANONYMOUS

I f a dog jumps up into your lap,

it is because he is fond of you; but if

a cat does the same thing,

it is because your lap is warmer.

ALFRED NORTH WHITEHEAD

Should ever anything be missed—
milk, coals, umbrellas, brandy
—The cat's pitched into with a boot
or anything that's handy.

C. S. CALVERLEY

Ding, dong, bell
Pussy's in the well.
Who put her in?
Little Johnny Green.
Who pulled her out?
Little Tommy Stout.
What a naughty boy was that
To try to drown poor pussy cat,
Who never did him any harm,
And killed the mice in his father's barn. ❧

NURSERY RHYME

It is with the approach of winter that cats . . . wear their richest fur and assume an air of sumptuous and delightful opulence.

PIERRE LOTI

I have found my love of cats most helpful in understanding women.

JOHN SIMON

CAT 🐾 FACT

"HEY, WHAT ARE YOU LOOKING AT?"

Cats take personal hygiene very seriously.
Some cats will not urinate if their litter box is
in a noisy area. Like humans, felines like
privacy and quiet in their bathrooms.
But cats never complain about people
leaving the seat up.

Cats mean kittens,
plentiful and frequent.

DORIS LESSING

Unlike us, cats never outgrow their delight in cat capacities, nor do they settle finally for limitations. Cats, I think, live out their lives fulfilling their expectations.

IRVING TOWNSEND

A plate is distasteful to a cat,
a newspaper still worse; they like to eat
sticky pieces of meat sitting on a
cushioned chair or a nice Persian rug.

MARGARET BENSON

One cat just leads to another.

ERNEST HEMINGWAY

Six little mice sat down to spin,
Pussy passed by and she peeped in.
What are you doing, my little men?
Weaving coats for gentlemen.
Shall I come in and cut off your threads?
No, no, Mistress Pussy, you'd bite off our heads.
On, no, I'll not; I'll help you to spin.
That may be so, but you don't come in. ❧

NURSERY RHYME

When we caress her, she stretches herself, and arches her back responsively; but that is because she feels an agreeable sensation, not because she takes a silly satisfaction, like the dog, in faithfully loving a thankless master. 🐦

FRANÇOIS RENÉ DE CHATEAUBRIAND

Like a graceful vase,
a cat, even when
motionless, seems
to flow.

GEORGE F. WILL

CAT LORE

In Great Britain, some people believe that a sure remedy for a sty in the eye is a good rub with a tomcat's tail.

A house without
either a cat or a dog
is the house of
a scoundrel.

PORTUGUESE PROVERB

It is easy to understand why the rabble
dislike cats. A cat is beautiful;
it suggests ideas of luxury, cleanliness,
voluptuous pleasures.

CHARLES BAUDELAIRE

A cat cares for you only as a source of food, security, and a place in the sun. Her high self-sufficiency is her charm.

CHARLES HORTON COOLEY

CAT: A pygmy lion who loves mice, hates dogs, and patronizes human beings.

OLIVER HERFORD

Refined and delicate natures understand the cat. Women, poets, and artists hold it in great esteem, for they recognize the exquisite delicacy of its nervous system; indeed, only coarse natures fail to discern the natural distinction of the animal. 🐾

JULES CHAMPFLEURY

It's just an old alley cat that has followed us all the way home. It hasn't a star on its forehead, or a silky satiny coat. No proud tiger stripes, no dainty tread, no elegant velvet throat. It's a splotchy, blotchy city cat, not a pretty cat, a rough little bag of old bones. 'Beauty,' we shall call you. 'Beauty' come in. 🐦

EVE MERRIAM

I t is always diverting to find something . . . but to find a cat: that is unheard of! For you must agree with me that . . . even though it belongs to us now, it remains somehow apart, outside, and thus we always have:

$$\text{life} + \text{a cat.}$$

Which, I can assure you, adds up to an incalculable sum. 🐦

RAINER MARIA RILKE

A man has to work so hard so that something of his personality stays alive. A tomcat has it so easy, he has only to spray and his presence is there for years on rainy days.

ALBERT EINSTEIN

Dogs eat.
Cats dine.

❧

ANN TAYLOR

Thou art the Great Cat, the avenger of the Gods, and the judge of words, and the president of the sovereign chiefs and the governor of the holy Circle; thou art indeed . . . the Great Cat. ❧

INSCRIPTION ON THE ROYAL TOMBS AT THEBES

Cats, like men,
are flatterers.

WILLIAM S. LANDOR

As to Sagacity, I should say that his judgment respecting the warmest place and the softest cushion in a room is infallible, his punctuality at meal times is admirable, and his pertinacity in jumping on people's shoulders till they give him some of the best of what is going, indicates great firmness. ❧

THOMAS HENRY HUXLEY

The cat is, above all,
a dramatist.

MARGARET BENSON

Little Robin Redbreast sat upon a tree,
Up went the Pussy-cat, and down went he,
Down came Pussy-cat, away Robin ran;
Says little Robin Redbreast: "Catch me if you can!"

Little Robin Redbreast jumped upon a spade,
Pussy-cat jumped after him, and then he was afraid.
Little Robin chirped and sang, and what did Pussy say?
Pussy-cat said: "Mew, mew, mew," and Robin ran away. ❧

NURSERY RHYME

I f you want to be a psychological novelist

and write about human beings,

the best thing you can do is keep

a pair of cats.

ALDOUS HUXLEY

Some people say that cats are
sneaky, evil, and cruel.
True, and they have many other
fine qualities as well.

MISSY DIZICK

In my house you have to talk to cats because, being ten of them, there are a lot of important things you have to say to them—like "Get off" and "Shut up" and things like that.

BERYL REID

A cat is more intelligent than people believe, and can be taught any crime.

MARK TWAIN

Cats do care. For example, they know
instinctively what time we have to be
at work in the morning and they
wake us up twenty minutes before
the alarm goes off.

MICHAEL NELSON

366

Oh cat, I'd say, or pray: be—ootiful cat! Delicious cat! Exquisite cat! Satiny cat! Cat like a soft owl, cat with paws like moths, jewelled cat, miraculous cat! Cat, cat, cat, cat.

DORIS LESSING

The cat has a nervous ear,

that turns this way and that.

And what the cat may hear,

is known but to the cat.

DAVID MORTON

Some cats is blind,
And stone-deaf some,
But ain't no cat
Wuz ever dumb.

ANTHONY HENDERSON EUWER

Two things are
aesthetically perfect
in the world—the
clock and the cat.

ÉMILE AUGUSTE CHARTIER

The cat is
utterly sincere.

FERNAND MÉRY.

Cats are living adornments.

EDWIN LENT

There's no need for
a piece of sculpture in a
home that has a cat.

WESLEY BATES

The text of this book was set in

Bauer Text Initials and Evangel

by Harry Chester, Inc.

Book design by

Judith Stagnitto Abbate